alphabet

Inger
Christensen

alphabet

Translated
by Susanna Nied

A New Directions Book

Acknowledgments are due to the editors of the following publications in which extracts from this translation have appeared: *New Directions in Poetry and Prose*, *Out of Denmark*, *Poetry East*, *Poetry in Transit*, *Scandinavian Review*, *Spor* (Copenhagen), *Traces* (Paris), *Translation*.

Manufactured in the United States of America
New Directions Books are printed on acid-free paper
First published in the U.K. by Bloodaxe Books Ltd. First published as a New Directions Paperbook Original (NDP920) in 2001.
alphabet was first published in Danish—as *alfabet*—in 1981 by Gyldendal.
Published simultaneously in Canada by Penguin Books Canada Limited

Library of Congress Cataloging-in-Publication Data

Christensen, Inger, 1935-
   [Alfabet. English]
   Alphabet / Inger Christensen ; translated by Susanna Nied.
      p. cm
   ISBN 0-8112-1477-X (alk. paper)
   I. Nied, Susanna.   II. Title
   PT8176.13.H727 A4413 2001
   839.8'1174—dc21   00-066423

New Directions Books are published for James Laughlin
by New Directions Publishing Corporation
80 Eighth Avenue, New York 10011

Contents

TRANSLATOR'S NOTE

The length of each section of Inger Christensen's
alphabet is based on Fibonacci's sequence,
a mathematical sequence beginning 0, 1, 1, 2, 3, 5, 8,
13, 21..., in which each number is the sum of
the two previous numbers.

alphabet

1

apricot trees exist, apricot trees exist

2

bracken exists; and blackberries, blackberries;
bromine exists; and hydrogen, hydrogen

3

cicadas exist; chicory, chromium,
citrus trees; cicadas exist;
cicadas, cedars, cypresses, the cerebellum

4

doves exist, dreamers, and dolls;
killers exist, and doves, and doves;
haze, dioxin, and days; days
exist, days and death; and poems
exist; poems, days, death

5

early fall exists; aftertaste, afterthought;
seclusion and angels exist;
widows and elk exist; every
detail exists; memory, memory's light;
afterglow exists; oaks, elms,
junipers, sameness, loneliness exist;
eider ducks, spiders, and vinegar
exist, and the future, the future

6

fisherbird herons exist, with their grey-blue arching
backs, with their black-feathered crests and their
bright-feathered tails they exist; in colonies
they exist, in the so-called Old World;
fish, too, exist, and ospreys, ptarmigans,
falcons, sweetgrass, and the fleeces of sheep;
fig trees and the products of fission exist;
errors exist, instrumental, systemic,
random; remote control exists, and birds;
and fruit trees exist, fruit there in the orchard where
apricot trees exist, apricot trees exist
in countries whose warmth will call forth the exact
colour of apricots in the flesh

7

given limits exist, streets, oblivion

and grass and gourds and goats and gorse,
eagerness exists, given limits

branches exist, wind lifting them exists,
and the lone drawing made by the branches

of the tree called an oak tree exists,
of the tree called an ash tree, a birch tree,
a cedar tree, the drawing repeated

in the gravel garden path; weeping
exists as well, fireweed and mugwort,
hostages, greylag geese, greylags and their young;

and guns exist, an enigmatic back yard;
overgrown, sere, gemmed just with red currants,
guns exist; in the midst of the lit-up
chemical ghetto guns exist
with their old-fashioned, peaceable precision

guns and wailing women, full as
greedy owls exist; the scene of the crime exists;
the scene of the crime, drowsy, normal, abstract,
bathed in a whitewashed, godforsaken light,
this poisonous, white, crumbling poem

8

whisperings exist, whisperings exist
harvest, history, and Halley's

comet exist; hosts exist, hordes
high commanders, hollows, and within the hollows
half-shadows, within the half-shadows occasional

hares, occasional hanging leaves shading the hollow where
bracken exists, and blackberries, blackberries
occasional hares hidden under the leaves

and gardens exist, horticulture, the elder tree's
pale flowers, still as a seething hymn;
the half-moon exists, half-silk, and the whole
heliocentric haze that has dreamed
these devoted brains, their luck, and human skin

human skin and houses exist, with Hades
rehousing the horse and the dog and the shadows
of glory, hope; and the river of vengeance;
hail under stoneskies exists, the hydrangeas'
white, bright-shining, blue or greenish

fogs of sleep, occasionally pink, a few
sterile patches exist, and beneath
the angled Armageddon of the arching heavens, poison,
the poison helicopter's humming harps above the henbane,
shepherd's purse, and flax, henbane, shepherd's purse
and flax; this last, hermetic writing,
written otherwise only by children; and wheat,
wheat in wheatfields exists, the head-spinning

horizontal knowledge of wheatfields, half-lives,
famine, and honey; and deepest in the heart,
otherwise as ever only deepest in the heart,
the roots of the hazel, the hazel that stands
on the hillslope of the heart, tough and hardy,
an accumulated weekday of Angelic orders;
high-speed, hyacinthic in its decay, life,
on earth as it is in heaven

9

ice ages exist, ice ages exist,
ice of polar seas, kingfishers' ice;
cicadas exist, chicory, chromium

and chrome yellow irises, or blue; oxygen
especially; ice floes of polar seas also exist,
and polar bears, stamped like furs with their
identification numbers, condemned to their lives;
the kingfisher's miniplunge into blue-frozen

March streams exists, if streams exist;
if oxygen in streams exists, especially
oxygen, especially where cicadas'
i-sounds exist, especially where
the chicory sky, like bluing dissolving in

water, exists, the chrome yellow sun, especially
oxygen, indeed it will exist, indeed
we will exist, the oxygen we inhale will exist,
lacewings, lantanas will exist, the lake's
innermost depths like a sky; a cove ringed
with rushes, an ibis will exist,
the motions of mind blown into the clouds
like eddies of oxygen deep in the Styx

and deep in the landscapes of wisdom, ice-light,
ice and identical light, and deep
in the ice-light nothing, lifelike, intense
as your gaze in the rain; this incessant,
life-stylising drizzle, in which like a gesture
fourteen crystal forms exist, seven
systems of crystals, your gaze as in mine,
and Icarus, Icarus helpless;

Icarus wrapped in the melting wax
wings exists, Icarus pale as a corpse
in street clothes, Icarus deepest down where
doves exist, dreamers, and dolls;
the dreamers, their hair with detached
tufts of cancer, the skin of the dolls tacked together
with pins, the dryrot of riddles; and smiles,
Icarus-children white as lambs
in greylight, indeed they will exist, in-
deed we will exist, with oxygen on its crucifix,
as rime we will exist, as wind,
as the iris of the rainbow in the iceplant's gleaming
growths, the dry tundra grasses, as small beings

we will exist, small as pollen bits in peat,
as virus bits in bones, as water-thyme perhaps,
perhaps as white clover, as vetch, wild chamomile,
banished to a re-lost paradise; but the darkness
is white, say the children, the paradise-darkness is white,
but not white the same way that coffins
are white, if coffins exist, and not white
the same way that milk is white, if milk exists;
white, it is white, say the children,
the darkness is white, but not
white like the white that existed
when fruit trees existed, their blossoms so white,
this darkness is whiter; eyes melt

10

June nights exist, June nights exist,
the sky at long last as if lifted to heavenly
heights, simultaneously sinking, as tenderly as
when dreams can be seen before they are dreamed; a space
as if dizzied, as if filled with whiteness, an hourless

chiming of insects and dew, and no one in
this gossamer summer, no one comprehends that
early fall exists, aftertaste, afterthought;
just these reeling sets of restless ultrasounds
exist, the bat's ears of jade
turned toward the ticking haze;
never has the tilting of the planet been so pleasant,
never the zinc-white nights so white,

so defencelessly dissolved, gently ionized and
white, never the limit of invisibility so nearly
touched; June, June, your Jacob's ladders,
your sleeping creatures and their dreams exist,
a drift of galactic seed between
earth so earthly and sky so heavenly,
the vale of tears so still, so still, and tears
sinking, sinking like groundwater back

into earth; Earth; Earth in its trajectory
around the sun exists, Earth on its journey
along the Milky Way, Earth on its course with
its cargo of jasmine, jasper, iron,
iron curtains, omens, jubilation, Judas's kiss
kissed right and left, and virgin anger in
the streets, Jesus of salt; with the shadow of the
jacaranda over the river, with gyrfalcons, jet planes,
and January in the heart, with Jacopo della Quercia's
well Fonte Gaia in Siena and with July
heavy as a bomb, with domestic brains
heart defects, quaking grass and strawberries
the ironwood's roots in the earthworn earth

Earth sung by Jayadeva in his mystical
poem from the 12th century, Earth with
the coastline of consciousness blue, with nests where
fisherbird herons exist, with their grey-blue arching
backs, or where bitterns exist, cryptic
and shy, or night herons, egrets,
with the wingbeat variations of hedge sparrows, cranes
and doves; Earth exists with Jullundur, Jabalpur and
the Jungfrau, with Jotunheim, the Jura,
with Jabrun, Jambo, Jogjakarta,
with duststorms, Dutchman's breeches
with water and land masses jolted by tremors
with Judenburg, Johannesburg, Jerusalem's Jerusalem

atom bombs exist

Hiroshima, Nagasaki

Hiroshima, August
6th, 1945

Nagasaki, August
9th, 1945

140,000 dead and
wounded in Hiroshima

some 60,000 dead and
wounded in Nagasaki

numbers standing still
somewhere in a distant
ordinary summer

since then the wounded
have died, first many,
most, then fewer, but

all; finally
the children of the wounded
stillborn, dying

many, forever a
few, at last the
last; I stand in

my kitchen peeling
potatoes; the tap
runs, almost
drowning out the
children in the yard;

the children shout,
almost drowning out
the birds in the
trees; the birds
sing, almost

drowning out the whisper
of leaves in the wind;
the leaves whisper,
almost drowning
the sky with silence,

the sky with its light
and the light that almost
since then has recalled
atomic fire
a bit

11

love exists, love exists
your hand a baby bird so obliviously tucked
into mine, and death impossible to remember,
impossible to remember how inalienable
life, as easily as chemicals drifting
over the knotgrass and rock doves, all of it
is lost, vanishing, impossible to remember that
there and there flocks of rootless

people, livestock, dogs exist, are vanishing;
tomatoes, olives vanishing, the brownish
women who harvest them, withering, vanishing,
while the ground is dusty with sickness, a powder
of berries and leaves, and the buds of the caper
are never gathered, pickled with salt
and eaten; but before they vanish, before we
vanish, one evening we sit at the table with
a little bread, a few fish without cankers, and water
cleverly turned into water, one of
history's thousands of war paths suddenly
crosses the living room, you get up, limits,
given limits exist, streets, oblivion

everywhere, but your hideout comes no nearer
see the moon is too brightly lit and Charles's Wain
is going back empty as it came; the dead want
to be carried, the sick want to be carried, the broken
pale soldiers looking like Narcissus want to
be carried; you wander around in such a strangely
endless way; only when they die do you stop
in a kale patch no one has tended for several
centuries, follow the sound of a dried-up
spring, somewhere in Karelia maybe, and as
you think of words like chromosomes and chimeras
and the aborted growth of lychees, fruits of love,
you peel off some tree bark and eat it

somewhere I am suddenly born
in an expressionless house; when you
cry out the walls give way and

the garden, in which you vanish, is
worn smooth by slugs; you bathe
jerking like a bird, and when the earth

is eaten and the rhubarb first
dries up, summer gives way and
the town, in which you vanish, is

slow and black; you walk in
the streets, do as others do,
wordlessly in passing nudge

bits of brick into place; when the route
is tenacious, ingrained enough, the houses
give way, and the high plain spreads,

sullen, almighty, and almost
invisible; somewhere a wild
apricot tree stands still for a moment

and blooms, but just with a very
thin veil on the outspread branches
before going on regardless

fragment of a springtime, the kind
of evening when the roads lead almost
off into the blue, but no one
moves; the dust of the roads recalls
the dust of the roads where most
are shot and the silence
tugs at stones, but nothing happens

somewhere something no one has
touched tumbles from a shelf,
perhaps as my grandmother stands
as she always has stood in her
kitchen and cooks up dried apricots;
I know she is dead, but their scent
is so strong that the body sensing it

it becomes fruit itself; and as
the fruit is hung up in the nearest
tree, which may be a birch that
bears catkins, never apricots,
the shot sounds beforehand, ahead
of just after, its sound like a
door with no house standing wide open still

hydrogen bombs exist
a plea to die

as people used to die
one day in ordinary

weather, whether you
know you are dying
or know nothing, maybe

a day when as usual you have
forgotten you must die,
a breezy day in

November maybe, as
you walk into the kitchen
and barely manage to

notice how good
and earthy the potatoes
smell, and barely

manage to put the lid on,
wondering whether you
salted them before you
put the lid on,
and in a flash,

while puffs of steam
leak past the lid, barely
manage to remember your life
as it was and still
is, while the potatoes

boil and life, which you
always have said must go
on, really does go
on, a plea, an
ordinary plea, an

ordinary day, that
life can continue
completely ordinarily
without it ever happening
that any of all

the cruel experiments
that the Teller group
performed on
Eniwetok where
the waves of the
Pacific raged in fury,
or any of all
the experiments that

the Sakharov group
performed on
Novaya Zemlya where
the waves of the Arctic
Ocean raged in fury
without these
experiments or those
of the British French

Chinese ever reaching
real real-
isation here where we
still live in a
real real
world as opposed to
the unreality of
Novaya Zemlya

and Eniwetok; here I
walk down to the still
blue of the Sound shining
with evening, toss
a stone into the water,
see how the circles
widen, reaching
even the farthest shores

12

life, the air we inhale exists
a lightness in it all, a likeness in it all,
an equation, an open and transferable expression
in it all, and as tree after tree foams up in
early summer, a passion, passion in it all,
as if in the air's play with elm keys falling
like manna there existed a simply sketched design,
simple as happiness having plenty of food
and unhappiness none, simple as longing
having plenty of options and suffering none,
simple as the holy lotus is simple
because it is edible, a design as simple as laughter
sketching your face in the air

in mid-November, a season
when all human dreams are the same,
a uniform, blotted out history
like that of a sun-dried stone

a couple of mute parents stand there,
a dog and some children run round,
an arrival they try to imagine
as water that's raised to my mouth

I lay sleeping inside my hotel room;
it was like an alien dream
that the guest before me must have shouldered
aside in his sleep and forgot

in the dream there was no one familiar;
I met only the blank scrutiny
of an apricot tree in bloom, turning
around as it left suddenly

perhaps it was left there one summer
when the world was as white as a feast,
before I had learned that a dreamer
must dream like the trees, be a dreamer
of fruit to the last

snow
is not snow at all
when it snows
in mid-June

snow has
not fallen from
the sky at all
in June

snow itself
has risen
and has bloomed
in June

as apple
apricot
chestnut trees
in June

to be lost
in real snow
which is June snow
in flower and seed

when you need never die

don't panic; it's bracken on a
trip, gathering time and
binding it; bracken has

its own calendar, tears and rain
and a little sunlight as black
as when black slugs carry it

around; ah, hear the tranquil
fronds and the undermost brown
seconds of the spores, ticking

still; perhaps they remember
how hidden we lay, how
hidden in places where

no people ever go we lay,
before we were born at last
and crept out; I look

back uneasily and the snow,
falling so thinly here this
morning, wakens carefully

and melts; a meadow lies
spread with lapwings; I walk
toward the sound; the ice

crackles icily, just as when
tears were once to be crushed
like pearls and strewn

over the patient; at last
the body is so salty that
its long story dissolves

the mirror; a little lint from a
quilt my mother must have shaken
disappears, and childhood

spreads ahead; over
by the window a little sunlight
is folded into place in the curtain

evening June sixteenth

from a train stopped too soon
I see that they're dumping
live coals outside
the closed brickworks

maybe as usual they're walking
down the path and away while
it gets ready to cloud up
and rain

only an edge of the farthest
fields is still in sun
so maybe it's not coals at
all that I see

maybe it's poppies, maybe
the closed brickworks is
a forest only partially
felled, maybe

it's sheep walking down
the path, while the shadows from
a fence they pass
toss in gusts

it's like looking
at an old painting whose
background is always being crossed
by a row of figures

not until it's all magnified
do you realise that they
are either people going home from
a brickworks

tired soldiers on the march
or sheep running away
from a herd; in the foreground
sits the Madonna

in a matted thicket
of green blackberries

cobalt bombs exist
wrapped in their cloaks
of cobalt-60 isotopes

whose half-life
ensures the most
harmful effects

there's no more to
say; we ensure that
the harm is as great
as it can be; there's no
more to say; we

ensure ourselves all or
nothing; there's no
more to say; by
ensuring that all
can be turned into

nothing, we
lose the capacity to
think of nothing,
of not a thing
in the world as we

say, when we simply
are being; there's
no more to
say; we
ensure

that it's all erased,
obliterated,
so the first
the crucial
nothing gets no chance
to make the poetry
that wind can make
in air or water;

there's no more
to say; we kill
more than we think
more than we know
more than we feel;
there's no more
to say; we hate;
there is no more;

like a regal bird
in its coffin of silt
in mud like a worm,
like a hawk
the storm has broken
like a grey parrot
dragged onto a steamboat
from someone's plantation

I'll live from now on
half-smothered, stuffed down
no one special among
all the traffic-worn doves
in whose last
clutch of feathers the hopeless
cloud cover of peace
makes the human eye

plummet; that's how I'll live;
with my own little fine
half-life deep in
my heart; that's how I'll die,
I have said to myself
I will die, said it with
thanks for sorrow,
oblivion, done; said
to myself: think like
a bird building nests,
think like a cloud, like
the roots of the dwarf birch

think; like a leaf on a tree
thinks; like shadow and light,
like shining bark thinks,
like the grubs beneath
the barkskin think, like lichen
on a stone and a bit of dry rot
think, like the squawroot thinks,
like this misty forest clearing
thinks, like the marshes think
where the rising of the rainbow
is reflected, think like a bit of
mud, a bit of raindrop
thinks, think like a mirror

so vitally — see
on its throne of nothing
the sandstorm's vortex;
see how banally enclosed
in the least small grain of
sand an ingenious
fossilised life rests up
from the trip; just see
how calmly it bears
the primal sea's swarm
of beginnings; just see
how simple a sign
in which like a substance

the truth is reflected;
just see how
truly, graciously; let
things be; add
words, but let
things be; see
how easily they find
shelter by themselves
behind a stone; see
how easily they steal
into your ear
and whisper
to death to go away

13

metal, the ore in the mountain, exists,

darkness in mine shafts, milk not let down
from mothers' breasts, an ingrown dread where

whisperings exist, whisperings exist
the cells' oldest, fondest collusion

consider this market, consider this import
and export of fathers, half bullies
half tortured soldiers, consider

their barren last vanishing, metal
to metal, as the amount of unsown maize
grows and the water shortage grows

speak now of mildness, now of the mystery
of salt; speak now of mediation, of mankind, of
courage; tell me that the marble of banks
can be eaten; tell me that the moon is lovely,
that the extinct moa eats green melon,

that merriment exists, is thriving,
that moss animals and mackerel shoals exist, that
means of giving up, of descent, exist, and
physical portioning out, as in poems, of matchless
earthly goods, that pity exists

layered light, as if behind
layers in a fresco the snow
on the mountains, its shapes

so like bromine dissolved
hidden as always on sleeptrips
a bit of sun breaks through as

if from the earthside, eggs
crack and quick as an eddy
of chaffinches over the hedge

the flight of thoughts from my
body; their aliveness, beaks,
wings, and the closeness

of the others' welcome as soon
as we alight on a birch and the
reason for our lives is revealed:

when the birches came to Lakselv
and founded the town they brought
along tufts of grass for a few sheep

so others than the leaves
could listen to the rustling
of the leaves and see how they

transform sunlight almost
as if to clear green water;
since then the sheep have sometimes

taken the birches along to the beach
a riddle for the reindeer at the
shoreline grazing

among half-furred stones, the last
bit of morning mist wrapped around
their greyish bodies, otherwise just

windless ice-turquoise sky
and the flower of an eider duck
on frost-stricken water

morning June twentieth

as if the hydrogen
at the stars' cores
turned white here on earth
your brain can
feel white

as if someone had
pleated up time
pushed it in
through the door of
a room

where a table
two chairs and the unused
bed of the non-sleeper
crumble
in advance

as if haze from
alien space
travelled like angels
you sit
in your corner

until without any-
thing definite happening
you suddenly
get up
and go

like a bird that
invisibly wakens
and feeds its
unborn young
at midnight

when no one can
know whether things
as they are
go on

it's new for me
        to be hearing cicadas
                here where it's cold
                        and so there are none

perhaps it's the kind
        of thing that's always happened
                when the light travels north
                        and the birches go along

like when a room from
        a dream on a trip
                is the same room that you
                        come home and move into

there's a drawing of
        an encapsuled child
                crouched inside a crystal
                        that's not especially big

as if in dreams
        dreamed not by people
                animals or birds
                        but by insects perhaps

perhaps by the traveller
        himself who is looking
                away from himself for a while
                        and is spread in the birches' haze

perhaps by a child who earnestly
      examines a lake in the forest
            and finds that the soul might well
                  have been dreamed by cicadas

it happens sometimes
      when the snow melts
            that all it has hidden
                  comes out so the soul can be seen

as when death doesn't really
      become visible until
            somebody looks at the gift
                  that the dead person took to the grave

I think it must look like
      he tarnished metal box
            I've known for a long time
                I'm carrying with me

it doesn't contain
      any more than a coin
            a tooth, a silver thimble
                and a little empty bottle

but its scent when
      it's opened
            fills everything
                like midnight sun

that's how I've imagined
        being able to imagine:
                a space of clear crystal
                        around the deathbed

where the dead person first
        really looks like himself
                by dying away from the others

following the sleepwalkers' trail now
on beneath the high plain's
broad balsam skies
across an icelocked lake
along a windgrown isle
straight down through the fire
straight out through the snow
wrapped in the cloak of the wind
baked in the bread of the sun
thwarted long-lasting precise
breathed into the stone-mountain's ice
over the grassblades' spires
under the root system's sores
out through the permafrost membrane
in through the iceplant's hairs
rechristened in mountain coal
cupped in the high tarn's eye
around a sunburst's arms
between a light-chasm's thighs
borne in the mountain king's jewel chest
exalted, select, and fine
preserved in the cradle of air
gone on the rainbow's paths
in through the shore lark's egg
out through the sunlight's wall
they silently travel
the Milky Way's dust
they set up their tents
in the leaves of the stars
the chicory blooms
so endlessly blue

as if no one were
anything except small
I sit myself down
with my wide-awake doll
whose eyes made of glass
are so strange and so fair
my mother comes out
with a steaming bowl
some meat she has warmed
at the North Star's fire
I talk with the doll
whose face looks like mine
about the good luck
that we cannot lose
so that we suddenly
are born, come to be
so that we all at once
meet others, increase
we borrow some fire
that's beginning to catch
as if we ourselves
had been rendered from death
as if even stars
at a touch could grow soft

defoliants exist
dioxin for instance
denuding trees and
shrubs and destroying
people and animals

by spraying
fields and forests
we achieve fall and death
in the middle of the most
luxuriant summer;

this shifting of sorrow
this light-filled morning
was otherwise happily fair
but the grass is all gone
and a canopy's spun
not of threads but of poisonous air
over forest and shore
over mouse over man

now the sky is a cavern
where withered birds
will rot like fallen fruit
where tractionless clouds
will atomise cities
and eddy them slyly in flight
like water through water
like sand through sand

even slugs with their slime-trails
are porous as mirrors
whose human reflections are lost
just the stalk of a nettle
explains leaflessly
that in our despair we have made
a flowerless earth
sexless as chlorine

see a morningpale star
gleams above like a brain
that is almost used up and burned out
too diffuse to recall
a man's and a woman's
union in their wingless flight
in a sweet-scented meadow
a summerwarm bed

see the clear waterfall
has congealed and grown small
on its way up the rock face again
and the fathomless roses
have hidden in bogs
indelible pollen laid by
for eternity
here they are copied fair in a script that is like
the script that the clouds in their drifting can write
or the script Archaeopteryx wrote into stone
across a dizzying sky-blue and clean
eternity
eternity

see the still becalmed wheat
in the haze and the heat
on its way down the rootstock again
while the poisonous winds
that paralyse blindly
move slowly and sullenly on
to eternity
never will death itself be the same any more
earthly death that all mortals must die as before
they are now counted down they are ticking away
while the earth crackles just as if it had frozen
for eternity
eternity

see the wonderful summer
the plums blue as doves
blown to particles feathering down
see the bindweed greywhite
as it crumbles and sinks
to the depths of the unmoulded clay
for eternity
there they are signed into the planless game
where none can tell whether a thing will remain
whether what's raven or starling or lark
lost for all time will find itself there
in eternity
eternity

while the leaves of an elm tree
are swept down a street
and summer is greying with soot
I walk down the avenue
dark as when snow
one evening has frozen to blood
for eternity
here I slip in behind an old graveyard's walls
where only the petrified doves go for walks
here they steal about in search of a place
where the stone heart informs them that peace settles down
for eternity
eternity

alphabets exist

the rain of alphabets

incessant rain

grace   light

intervals and forms
of stones of stars

courses of rivers and
motions of mind

tracks of animals
their routes and ways

nest-building
human solace

daylight in air
sign of the hawk

union in colour
of sunlight and eye

wild chamomile
at houses' doorsteps

snowbanks   wind
house corners   sparrows

I write like wind
that writes with clouds'
tranquil script

or quickly across the sky
in vanishing strokes
as if with swallows

I write like wind
that writes in water
with stylised monotony

or roll with the heavy
alphabet of waves
their threads of foam

write in air
as plants write
stalks and leaves

or loopingly as with flowers
in plumed circles
filaments   dots

I write like the water's edge
writes a tideline
of seaweed and shells

or delicately as mother of pearl
feet of starfish
secretions of mussels

I write like the early
spring that writes
the common alphabet
of anemones beeches
violets wood-sorrel

I write like childlike
summer like thunder
over domed treetops
whitegold of ripening
lightning and wheat

I write like autumn
marked for death
like restless hopes
lightstorms slicing
fog   memory

I write like winter
write like snow
and ice and cold
darkness   death
write

I write like the beating
heart writes
the skeleton the nails
the teeth the hair
the skull their silence

I write like the beating
heart writes
the hands the feet
the skin the lips
the sex their whisper

I write like the beating
heart writes
the muscles the lungs
the face the brain
the nerves their sound

I write like the beating
heart writes
the blood the cells
the visions the tears
the tongue their cry

14

nights exist, nightshade exists
the dark side, the cloak of namelessness exists

the northern limits of consciousness exist, there
where what is dreamed opens and closes its
northerly crown in nastic turnings

without day and night being definitely
placed, without nadir, zenith
straight below or above and without

the naos, the innermost space of the cell
revealing whether the seed in an inner sky
gathers the limits of consciousness into a point
a flowering point where like a bit of sunshine
ice ages exist, ice ages exist

where like a bit of fire the insects' wingless
Nike exists, neither victory nor
defeat, just the solace of nothing;
the solace of names, that nothing has
a name, namelessness has a name

that names exist, names like narwhal
nettle, names like carnation, tawny owl
and nightjar, names like nightingale, new moon
evening primrose, naiads, and the other kind of
name in which a word when named is scent
like the narwhal's name for Arctic seas,
the nettles' names for fever, like carnations'

names for light reflected into factory-white
nights, like the tawny owl's, the nightjar's names
for feathers, the nightingale's names for being
an Old World warbler hidden in moist thickets
like the new moon's names for Earth and Sun
the evening primrose family's names for kinship
like the naiads' names for being pondweed
whispering the naiads' names in wind

so here I stand by the	Barents Sea
out there is the	Barents Sea
and it looks like the	Barents Sea
is always alone with the	Barents Sea
but around behind the	Barents Sea
the water stops at	Spitzbergen
and just behind	Spitzbergen
ice drifts in the	Arctic Ocean
and just behind the	Arctic Ocean
there's solid ice at the	North Pole
and just behind the	North Pole
it looks like the	Beaufort Sea
is all alone with the	Beaufort Sea
but around in back of the	Beaufort Sea
it looks like	Alaska
has always seen only	Alaska
but behind	Alaska
at last is the	Pacific Ocean
it looks like the	Pacific Ocean
is always alone with the	Pacific Ocean
but around behind the	Pacific Ocean
ice drifts in the	Antarctic Ocean
and just behind the	Antarctic Ocean
there's solid ice at the	South Pole
and just behind the	South Pole
there's water again in the	South Atlantic
and just behind the	South Atlantic
the water stops at	Africa
and just behind	Africa
some water again in the	Mediterranean
and just behind the	Mediterranean

it looks like	Turkey
is all alone with	Turkey
but around in back of	Turkey
there's water again in the	Black Sea
and just behind the	Black Sea
it looks like	Romania
is always alone with	Romania
but right behind	Romania
there's the	Soviet Union
it looks like the	Soviet Union
is all alone with the	Soviet Union
but right behind the	Soviet Union
there's	Finland
looking like	Finland
is all alone just	Finland
but around behind	Finland
there's	Finnmark
and just behind	Finnmark
there's the	Barents Sea
planed and chrome plated	
beneath a dome of light	
so here I stand by the	Barents Sea
all alone by the	Barents Sea
evening June 24th	

the Gävle canal is as shiny as metal
and regardless of weather it always reflects
a cloud cover somewhere, so you never
feel up to carving your heart in
the water and, blindly as a poem that
is written too soon, flowing away
from the county extras in the square

the streets lie as someone must have
laid them out once, waiting, the light from
pavements rises toward an overgrown sky
and not until five o'clock when the factory gate
opens do you see a child run over to
her father while he looks like a stranger
and share his uneasiness before it disappears

it is here in a worn-down province
where from hour to hour the street-trees
cast shadows longer than before
collect water and watch that the adults
keep track of their allotted time
and preferably feel no regret

it is here in a worn-down province
where no citrus trees bloom
where the swallows do not even come and
summer is almost somber with sun
that people lie awake and think
while the gardens slowly take root

only a few dogs are still about
an eagle lands on a coverlet of
air, while a child in her bed gets
the printed wallpaper to look like
a sky that will clear up soon

it is here in a worn-down province
with a wistfulness no one dares love
that the gravel on the paths of the manor grounds
keeps creaking for years
after the last lovers have gone away

it is here in a worn-down province
that the last flock of houses has long
since stopped so people can watch TV
and save up tears for future use

only a nestless sparrow flutters up into the air
only a breath as if from everything's
lawless sorrow makes a tree
whisper a black indefinite sound

before the train starts up with a jerk
and I soon will remember only the
empty platform and the bench with the

wet newspaper, which the wind,
leafing so pensively through everything, never
could lift, while the rest is washed into

my childhood somewhere in a
dry indestructible house where

I stand by a window and look
at the train through the sheets of rain

evening June sixteenth

there's something specific
            about the doves' way
                  of living my life
                        as a natural result

of today since it's raining
            and as always in rain
                  they softly alight
                        on the window ledge

so close to the white
            piece of paper that they
                  can easily see if
                        I'm writing of doves or of rain

it can feel wrong
            that it never is doves
                  themselves impassively
                        writing of doves

of the rain perhaps
            or the pane that they just
                  with a round little eye
                        see me so blurrily through

they don't realise
            that especially their flight
                  and their wings are connected
                        with gentleness, peace

a relationship making it
		practically impossible
				to mention doves as doves
						for instance in a poem

or to mention doves in rain
		as the drenched and dishevelled
				doves in rain that they are
						today since it's raining

it was actually first
		at Berlevåg's harbour
				where the gulls rage
						in the cold in June

that the absence of doves
		of their arbitrary
				clucking and crooning
						struck me with something

that was not wonder
		but quite ordinary
				everyday openness
						almost a reverence

as if the world held
		a magnificent crystalline sphere
				of minuscule steps
						on wine-red feet

an ever-enamoured
		complex tracking-down
				of food and desire
						in the caverns of day

a murmuring wanting
      from second to second
           to circumvent death
                and communicate presence

it struck me that poems
      about doves about rain
           must start in an egg
                in a dizzying drop

must start out with down
      with a gathering of drops
           with feather on feather
                a searched-out design

with greyish and brownish
      and whitish and bluish
           immaculate colours
                with strata of water in air

with a heart somewhere
      with delicate lungs
           like bracken of oxygen
                with the clouds' web

with absence and at
      the same time with a thirst
           for human happiness
                with all the possible

words made impossible
      meaningless so that
           the rain can rain down
                and the doves can alight

so softly upon
      the white paper that I
            can easily see if they're
                  writing of me or of you

of the rain perhaps
      or the peace that they just
            with a round little eye
                  see us so blurrily through

morning June 26th

dreamers go around openly now
with dreams out on their skin

with the lustre of membranes
and entrails spread over

their bodies like old-fashioned
maps; the specific

contours of the moment show
the future's embryo

as a contagious stand of fossils
and the earth's surface cracks like

peeling canvas; the stuff
of dreams and everything else a human

being was made of flutters
in the air, a few classic

strips of veil and gauze
around the glassclear thoughts

while drops of sorrow break out
on a forehead washed clean;

as when ships with windblown
dead leave the sinking

water and put in through the town
in the creeping sun they always

gather on a summer-grey evening
with violence and decency

bound to fragile flesh like
particles of soot bound to soap;

anyone at all is a hostage
somewhere in the jungle of consciousness

and builds on a church of snow
anyone at all raves on about

the gods' punishment about chaos
that reaches its boiling point far

too soon and anyone at all
curries favour unseen

with the patrols of an unyielding order
where they hand over life as collateral;

only the poor live on in fear
of dying before the rich give

orders at last for
anything at all;

and as clocks run races over
the planet and hearts are filled with

stone after stone that never will
fall as machines devise

other machines as if it were
possible to conceal that the future

conceals nothing today as
nothing happens as I sit

somewhere in my apartment almost
apathetic alone at any rate with

thirty pounds of white paper today
as August eleventh slowly

but surely vanishes as
the full moon closes its eyes

against the dazzling sun today
a woman returns to

the village sees if there is
water in the charred

well grubs a bit in the ground
with a stick but picks up

nothing and sits down and
waits thinks she can hear

a dog in the distance from
the forest that's still smoking

and that keeps on smoking
when the night chill comes

thinks she can hear the stars'
flames when the stars come out

right where the house with
the fence and garden used to be

thinks she'll rest
a bit and dies

a bird flies off a bit of dust
eddies up a drop of water falls

on a leaf on a branch on a tree
on an earth and the rain starts

to cry noted somewhere in the
distance as rain on the computer

screen a bit of infrared radiation
from the forest that's still smoking

is irrelevant and radiation
from moving animals does not show up

a group of children seeks shelter in a cave
mutely observed only by a hare

as if they were children in childhood's
fairy-tales they hear the wind tell

of the burned-off fields
but they are no children

no one carries them any more

INGER CHRISTENSEN was born in 1935. She is one of Denmark's best-known poets, and has published six books of poetry over a forty-year period. She has also written novels, plays, children's books and essays. As well as winning many Danish awards, she has won several major European literary awards, including the prestigious Nordic Prize of the Swedish Academy (1994), Der österreichische Staatspreis für Literatur (1994), Preis der Stadt Münster für Europäische Poesie (1995) and Grand Prix des Biénnales Internationales de Poésie (1996).

Inger Christensen has been a member of Det Danske Akademi (the Danish Academy) since 1978, of the Bielfelder Colloquium since 1994, and of the Académie Européene de Poésie since 1996.

SUSANNA NIED is a former instructor of English and comparative literature at San Diego State University in California. Her work has appeared in various literary journals and anthologies. Her translation of *alphabet* won the 1982 ASF/PEN Translation Prize for Poetry, awarded by the American-Scandinavian Foundation and *Scandinavian Review*.